THE NUMBER STORY

BOOK ONE

Numbers Teach Children
Their Number Names

written and illustrated by
MISS ANNA

LP LUMPY PUBLISHING

For my children,
David, Samuel,
John and Daniel
May you love to learn and learn to love.
And
For my husband

Who encourages me to pursue my dreams

We are Numbers.

You have seen us before
Around your house and in stores.

We are on toys,

in books,

on birthday cards,

on crooks.

We are important you see.
And each of us has a name, like Three.

We know you may think it's a hard game
To connect us with the right name.

So we Numbers thought of a way
For you to remember our names

starting

today.

Are you ready?

Good. Yay!

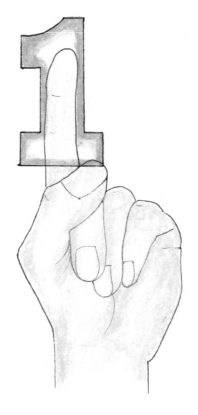

1   looks like my one finger.

2 trails a tail.

3 has bumps.

4 carries a sail.

5 is a racing track. *Vroom!*

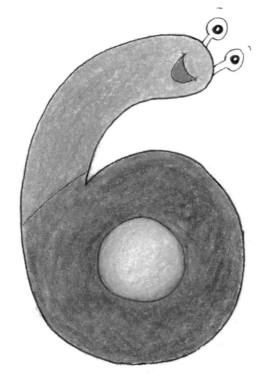

6 curves like a snail.

7 has a sharp angle.

8 is rollercoaster rails. *Yippee*

9 is a bubble on top of a stick.

And

10 is one eye of a whale.

How about zero?

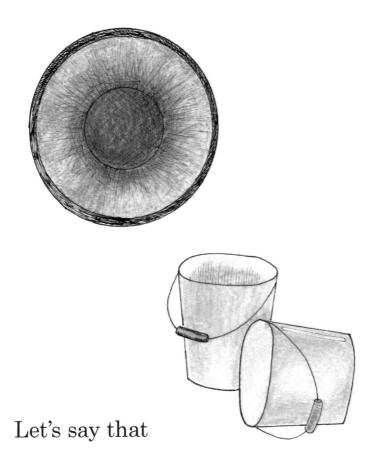

Let's say that

0 is an empty pail.

You have been so
kind to listen to
our story.

Remembering our
names is easy,
Not to worry.

Call us with the right names.
Make it a game.
Our hearts excitedly tingle
When you remember our jingle.

So here we go again
Before we say toodle-oo.

But this is not a goodbye. It's true.
Everywhere, all around you,
We Numbers will be waving at you.

"Do you see us? *Yoo-hoo!*"

Numbers! Numbers! In order please.

 1 looks like my one finger.

 2 trails a tail.

 3 has bumps.

 4 carries a sail.

5 is a racing track. *Vroom!*

 6 curves like a snail.

7 has a sharp angle.

 8 is rollercoaster rails. *Yippee*

 9 is a bubble on top of a stick.

 And
10 is one eye of a whale.

How about zero?

 Let's say that
0 is an empty pail.

Library of Congress Control Number: 2016913243

Woo, Jieeun, author, illustrator.
[Works. Selections]
The number story 1 : Numbers teach their names ;
The number story 2 : Numbers teach to count / written
by Jieeun Woo ; illustrated by Jieeun Woo.
  pages cm
Titles from separate title pages; works issued
back-to-back and inverted (tête-bêche format).
SUMMARY: In "Number story 1," the numbers show
children a creative way to connect the numerical name to
the right numerical symbol. In "Number story 2," the
numbers count with children to show 1-to-1
correspondence between the numerical symbol and the act
of counting.
Audience: Ages 2-5.
ISBN 978-0-9962164-8-7

1. Numeration--Juvenile literature. 2. Number
concept--Juvenile literature. 3. Numbers, Natural--
Juvenile literature. 4. Counting--Juvenile literature.
5. Upside-down books. [1. Number systems. 2. Number
concept. 3. Numbers, Natural. 4. Counting.
5. Upside-down books.] I. Container of (work): Woo,
Jieeun. Number story 1. II. Container of (work): Woo,
Jieeun. Number story 2. III. Title. IV. Title: Number
story 2.

QA141.3.W66 2016   513.5
                     QBI16-900037

Publisher: Lumpy Publishing
website www.missannabooks.com.
Email. tomissanna@gmail.com
Facebook. Miss Anna Lumpy

Paperback: ISBN 978-0-9962164-8-7
Hardback: ISBN 978-0-9962164-9-4

Printed in the U.S.A.   5 7 9 10 8 6

Author Bio

Miss Anna (Jieeun Jeanne Woo)

Let us write.
Let us draw.
Let us create for all.
Learning should be fun.
The half-steps have begun.
Oh to see them smile, lil' ones big and small.

— Miss Anna

MISS ANNA writes for her four boys.
They are her inspiration to present knowledge
in new, creative ways—ways that will help
knowledge stay. She writes from her home in
the beautiful and green Portland, Oregon.

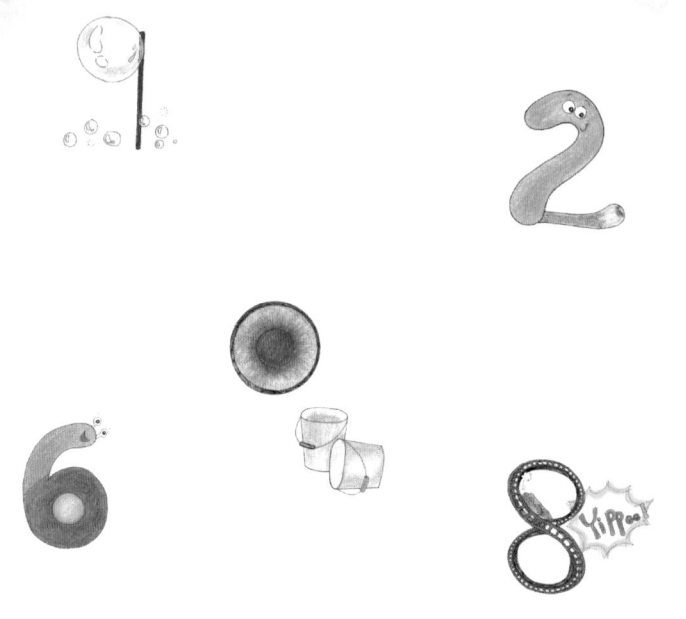

Do you remember our Number names?

Call our names anytime.

Match the names with
our pictures in rhymes.

Count with us. It is a game you must play.

ONE LOOKS LIKE MY ONE FINGER ♪

TWO TRAILS A TAIL ♪

Learning is fun when you can see
We Numbers in our creative spree.
You will see us again very soon
Saying our names in a happy tune.

7 Puzzles

8 Pins

9 Trumpets

10 Tins

And

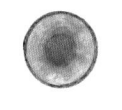

0 Zins

1 Fire Truck

2 Twins

3 Baseballs

4 Bins

5 Feathers

6 Fins

Zins?
We know. Zins is not a word.
It is nothing, *zilch*, zip!
We just wanted to see you grin.

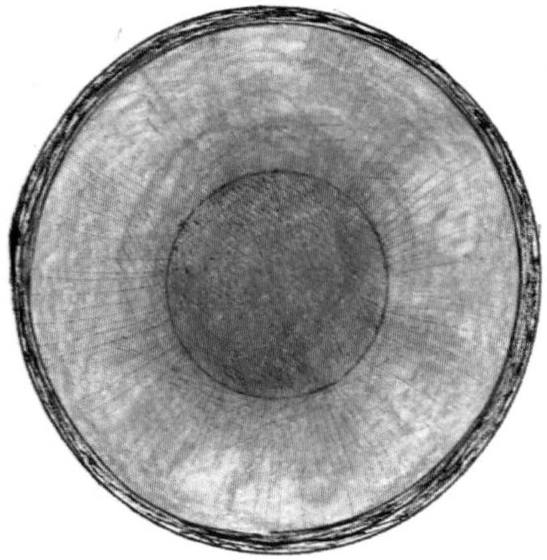

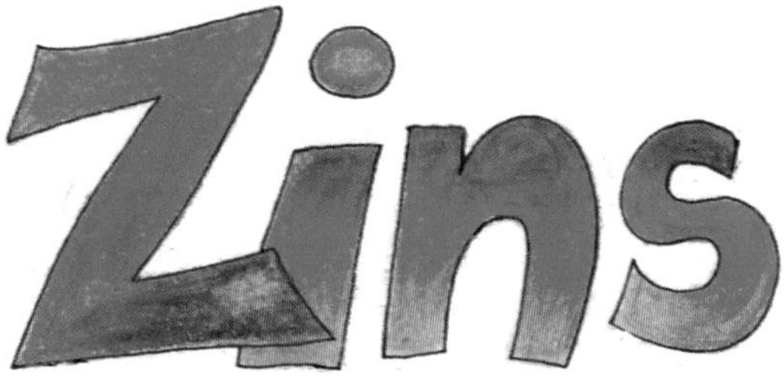

And 0 Zins

9 Trumpets

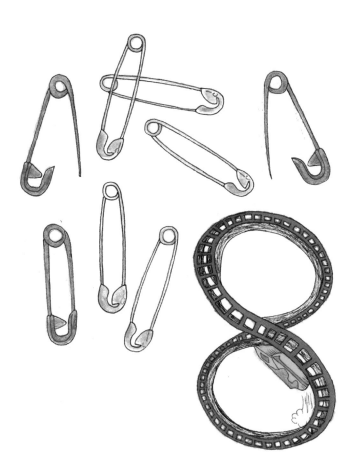

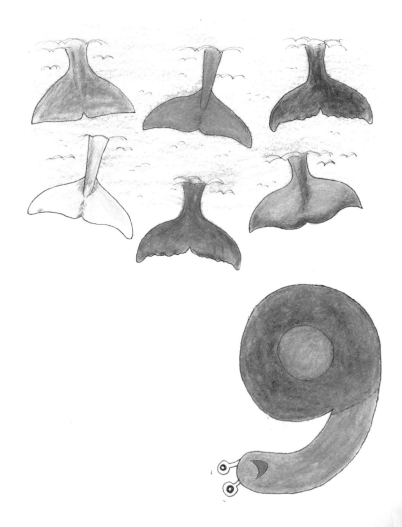

5 Feathers

4 Bins

3 Baseballs

2 Twins

1

Fire Truck

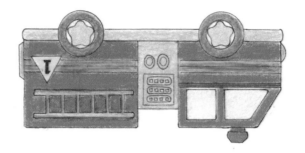

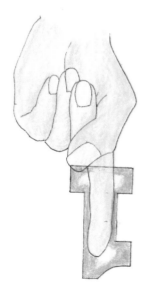

The counting game has now started.
Whoopee!

Come count with us — one, two, three.

Counting from zero to ten
Is our favorite one.

Our names with our pictures
Are used for much fun.

We are Numbers.

You have seen us before.
With you we have another activity in store.

For my children,
David, Samuel,
John and Daniel
May you live to love and love to live.

THE NUMBER STORY

BOOK TWO

Numbers Count with Children

written and illustrated by
MISS ANNA

LP LUMPY PUBLISHING

CPSIA information can be obtained at www.ICGtesting.com
Printed in the USA
BVIW12n0029190917
495002BV00013B/25